Unleashed

Unleashed

Climbing Canines,
Hiking Hounds, Fishing Fidos,
and Other Daring Dogs

LISA WOGAN

SKIPSTONE

INTRODUCTION

When Wrigley sprints down the dock near her Mercer Island, Washington, home, dozing ducks and geese flutter off in every direction. At full speed, she leaps off the end and—stretched like a smile, the wind whistling through webbed paws—she snatches a T-ball in mid-air before splashing down and swimming it back to her right-hand man Todd Butson. It is a display of beauty and athleticism that could move Greg Louganis to share one of his four gold medals.

But the seven-year-old chocolate Labrador retriever (on the cover) is no pro. She's never competed in diving or agility competitions. Her elegant belly flops are all just a day in the park—where she runs, retrieves, and swims, with her Lab buddy Roanoke, until she's exhausted. Thanks to a mix of DNA, training, and pleasure, Wrigley transforms a simple walk along the shore into something delightful.

Our dogs can't tell us why they are thrilled by certain things, why gnarly sticks, mud puddles, or big waves rock their world. We speculate about predator drive and genetics and training, but all we really know from watching them is how much there is out there to be enjoyed. Like a translator or a guide, they shed light on the outdoors. It's an ideal arrangement. When we bring our dogs along for our favorite adventures and theirs, they get the big-time fun and exercise they need and we get the prancing, splashing, and snorting that paints the world in Technicolor.

Of course, it's not always easy. We have to make space for our dogs on a bike, board, or boat. Buy tennis balls by the gross. Stock up on booties. Plan vacations with our dogs' special passions in mind. Drive when we could fly. Pack extra water and coats. Stop when they are hot or tired. We even modify our vocabulary, only using words like surf, fish, swim, or Frisbee when we are absolutely, just-that-moment going to surf, fish, swim, or play Frisbee. If we're making plans, we resort to spelling words or using just the first letter—all of which our dogs fully understand. We do everything we can to protect them, and know if they get hurt out there, we'll do everything we can to fix them up.

In exchange, they coax us out of our armchairs. They prod us to run a little faster, hike a little longer, and play a little wilder. When they refuse to drop an unmanageable log or decide to retrieve rocks from the bottom of a river, they make us laugh. When they jam down a mountain in a wheelchair or scale boulders on six-inch legs, they inspire us. They help us to feel safe in unfamiliar places and give us courage to tackle new experiences. They remind us that there is soul-quenching, full-body-rolling pleasure to be had from the most basic natural elements such as grass, mud, snow, water, and sun.

Unleashed celebrates the hiking hounds, climbing canines, fishing fidos, and other daring dogs who know how to have a good time—a really good time—in the outdoors, in a way that helps us to do the same.

SPORT: EXTREME SPRINKLER
DOG: MOE

· · · · ·

If Moe the Welsh terrier
came with instructions, they might read:
Jumping Bean—just add water.

The two-year-old wirehair pup whirls in the spray of a backyard sprinkler as if he just lapped up a bowl of Jolt Cola. Dodging and weaving through the streams of water, he tries to gather them in his mouth. At a dizzying pace, he pogoes on his hind legs, rebounding off the side of the house and the fence, all to the tune of his own deafening bleats.

Meryl Carver-Allmond discovered Moe's passion for fountain-crashing while gardening in her Lawrence, Kansas, backyard. One day he attacked the hose with great zeal while she watered her vegetable plot. His pleasure was so pure she rewarded him with a sprinkler and then shot a video so manic it's sure to be a YouTube hit. For a time, Moe tried joining Meryl for her morning showers only to learn Extreme Sprinkler is not an indoor sport.

SPORT: SKIJORERS
DOGS: CORSA BELLA, TUDOROSE EUREKA! GOLD MINE, BIBELOT'S TOLKA TINTANIUM, & ALCHMYS MAGIC TIN NICK-L BLUES

· · · · ·

It's hard to imagine what Jack London would have made of Corsa, TinTin, Eureka, and Nickel—four elegantly groomed, purebred standard poodles zooming through snowy forests with jingle bells on their collars and, in the case of TinTin and Eureka, towing a woman on skate skis.

"Snowmobilers can't figure it out," Vikki Kauffman says about her poodle-powered version of skijoring, a Scandinavian sport that combines mushing with cross-country skiing. Contrary to their effete reputation, poodles are strong, tough dogs. They gather steam in the harness, and on corners Vikki can feel like the last skater in a game of Crack the Whip.

She has always been a dedicated outdoorswoman and climber. But when her husband died in an avalanche ten years ago, Vikki had a hard time returning to the natural world they had enjoyed together. "I couldn't even go for a hike because Phil was my soul mate and our passion was the outdoors," she says.

A little more than one year after her husband's death, she rescued Corsa Bella, a one-year-old black standard poodle, who had spent her first year in a barn with almost no human-social interaction. It took two years for Corsa to allow anyone other than Vikki to touch her.

"I think her sensitivity and her needing me so much really helped me get out of myself," Vikki says. Corsa also helped Vikki return to the backcountry and eventually try skijoring six years ago. "On the trail, Corsa would go off and come back and say, 'This is wonderful. Come share this with me,'" Vikki explains.

"She saved my life. At least, she saved my soul."

SPORT: FLY-FISHERDOG
DOG: PWINCE TASSELHOFF BURFOOT

· · · · ·

Surfacing for mayflies, a hungry cutthroat trout is suddenly the subject of dreamy brown eyes, peering down an impossibly long nose framed by enormous earflaps. Before the poor fish can complete a double take, the water vibrates with a sonorous woof.

Tasselhoff Burfoot is fishing. When the basset hound sees his quarry, he barks, catches the eye of Mary Mischelle Kemp, who stands midstream, and then stares back at the precise spot of the trout's hurried dive.

"It's like 'Mom, it's right there,'" Mary says. "It's crazy." But after eight years fishing Utah's rivers with Tas, she knows better than to doubt him.

Bassets have a rep as couch potatoes, but somewhere in those bones is a passion for the outdoors. In Tas's case that passion takes the form of catching (with Mary's "help") and sometimes eating rainbow, cutthroat, and brook trout. "He'll watch when I reel the fish in. If I lose it, he gives me this look of disgust," Mary says.

A lifelong fisherwoman, Mary knew from the start

Tas would join her on river outings, but she never imagined he'd be an active participant. "When I caught a fish, he would go crazy," says Mary, who generally follows a catch-and-release policy. "One time I thought, I wonder what he'll do with it. So I chucked it to him. He just went nuts. That's when he learned to read the water."

Mary sticks to smaller rivers, where she can easily keep an eye on Tas and his sidekick Fizban. It may be counterintuitive, but she thinks bassets' dislike for water is what makes them good riverside companions. "With those big dense bones and little short legs, they're like the Titanic. They sink," she says. "It's perfect for a fishing dog because they don't jump in the water much."

SPORT: SNOWSHOER
DOG: KEROUAC

· · · · ·

The shurriip of Velcro in another room will wake Kerouac out of a deep sleep.
He knows Velcro equals gloves and boots. Which, in turn, equals snow, squirrels, dead stuff,
and a million other backcountry delicacies. It's Pavlovian.

"Kerouac hears Velcro and he comes charging at me, like, 'what's goin' on?'" says Scott Quibell, who has been roaming British Columbia's forests and meadows with his furry pal for eight years. Depending on the season, Kerouac joins Scott on hikes, trail runs, mountain-bike rides, and snowshoe or cross-country ski tours almost daily in wilderness a mere five blocks from their Kamloops home. They have watched, a little nervously, as a mountain lion tracked their progress. Spied moose during snowy moonlight outings. Even faced off silently with a bear they spooked in the middle of a trail.

The floppy-eared, German shepherd mix earned his stripes in outdoor survival early on. A friend of Scott's discovered the skinny young stray living off the land and garbage along a river in town. It took some time to coax him back to civilization and eventually into Scott's life. Today they are inseparable, except for the few times that thunder sends Kerouac out a door or window on a frightened walkabout.

After each mini-expedition, Kerouac, who hasn't been on a leash in five years, crawls up on the couch while Scott reads. "He puts his head up on my lap and falls asleep," Quibell says. "It's a perfect friendship."

SPORT: SYNCHRONIZED SWIMMER
DOG: GUS

· · · · ·

*Almost every day in the summertime, Sally Oien plunges
into Lake Washington for a long swim.*

She grew up splashing across Wisconsin lakes and never lost her love of floating uninterrupted distances in fresh water. For most of her life, she's been out there by herself with the waves, the big fish, and the slimy plants, which shows some courage because big fish and slimy plants give her the serious creeps.

Her solo status changed nine years ago, when Gus, her then two-year-old Border collie mix, spontaneously decided it was time to leave the beach and come along. (Gus is a female named for Augustus McCrae, Robert Duvall's character in *Lonesome Dove*.) Today,

they swim as much as a mile in sync. When Sally lifts her head from the water to take in big gulps of air, she's only inches from Gus's steadfast profile.

A shy, leggy beauty with long, silky, black fur and white boots, Gus has always just seemed to know what to do. Her dog paddle makes scarcely a ripple. She never crawls up on Sally, just swims in tandem. "If she wants to stop, she puts her front paws on my arm and lets her back legs hang," Sally says. "She knows I'll keep her afloat out there in the deep."

SPORT: MARATHONER
DOG: MISS DAISY ONE DOT

• • • • •

Running has always been Miss Daisy's style. On the way home from the pound, she slithered over the shoulder of her newly minted guardian Dave Swenson and bolted out the door. "I thought two things," Dave says. "One, that's the fastest dog I have ever seen. And two, there goes a hundred bucks."

It was the first time, but it wouldn't be the last. "That was part of her charm; she kept running away," says Dave, an economics researcher in Ames, Iowa. Because his four-year-old rat terrier has an ornery streak when it comes to other dogs, he found a nearly fool-proof method for tracking her down post-escape. "I just turn the radio off and roll the window down and listen for barking dogs."

Eventually, he decided to focus all that energy into something more constructive and mutual—marathons. A runner for about ten years, Dave has completed more than ninety marathons, including one in each state, plus a couple dozen ultramarathons. Using a 5-foot leash, he trained Daisy like a marathoner—increas-

ing her distance and building strength over time. After two years, she won the canine division at the Central States Marathon and the Wyoming Marathon. (OK, so she was the sole entrant in her division both times.)

She recently joined what has to be the very elite ranks of ultramarathoning dogs. It wasn't easy. At mile 27 of the Fat Ass 50K in Cameron, Missouri, she shot Dave a dubious look, which he took to mean, "Dave, let's go back." He slowed their pace. At mile 29, she pulled him toward a sunny knoll, which roughly translated to "Let's take a nap." They stopped and he gave her a little massage. She bounced back, however, and they trotted over the finish line at mile 31 in six hours and twenty-two minutes.

SPORT: **SURFER**
DOG: **BUDDY**

• • • • •

The marvel of Buddy begins on dry land. The moment he sees his boogie board,
he goes ballistic: kicking up sand, barking, leaping at the board, and chomping the edges.

His frenzy draws sunbathers out of loungers and dogs onto beachfront balconies along his home beaches in Ventura, California. No witness is ever disappointed. Bruce Hooker, Buddy's number one *brah*, slides the board (which after years of dog love looks like a shark's pacifier) into the surf. Buddy jumps on as it skims back and forth. He shifts his weight for stability and pirouettes when the board changes direction—all the while letting out machine-gun barks of glee. An eight-year-old Jack Russell terrier, he has been described as "a bleached, blow-dried possum."

After shredding the shallows, he often joins Bruce on an 11-foot soft-top board out among serious surfers. Buddy on the nose and Bruce on the tail. Out in the bigs—3- to 4-foot waves—he maintains his surfing poise. He always wears a floatation vest, because Buddy has taken some tough tumbles.

Buddy seemed destined for greatness. After his mother ate some rat poison during her pregnancy, he was the only puppy to survive. He started his sporting life as a runner, covering between 6 and 11 miles a day with Bruce's wife, Leslie. After a couple years, he was mighty fit but looking for a new challenge. During a family day at the beach, he spontaneously commandeered daughter Megan's boogie board and never looked back.

Bruce never used treats to coax Buddy into the waves. For Bruce—who is also tutoring Lola, the family's three-year-old Jack Russell, to hang 20—it's simple: "They have to want to do it."

SPORT: **MOUNTAIN BIKER**
DOG: **KAYA**

• • • • •

With no more warning than the ting of a bicycle bell, Kaya cranks around
a hairpin turn like a joy-filled maniac. Mudcicles hang from her shiny, penny-colored coat,
her muzzle is spattered with black flecks, and twigs are tangled in her feathery tail.
Hopping rocks close behind is avid mountain biker Mark Peterson.

At his "mush!" the eleven-year-old golden retriever bolts up the narrow track, flies over snags, balances on downed logs, and crashes through puddles. She runs ahead up hills—never out of view for long—and stays behind on the downhill. On tight transitions, she and Mark tango.

It looks like the perfect tandem fun, but it's not for every dog. "People don't really know a lot about riding with their dogs," says Mark, who is the president of the Bellingham, Washington, trail-riding association and works for Kona Bicycles, a mountain-bike manu-facturer. "You really have to be aware of them. If you ride too fast, they can overheat quickly and they'll push themselves to their limit before you even know it."

Kaya is in tip-top condition, but Mark always watches her for signs that she's slowing down and never takes her out when it's warm. Chilly, wet days are ideal. The mud slows his pace and keeps Kaya cool. Near the end of this day's ride, Mark has to stop to repair a flat. His partner takes advantage of the break to roll in wet leaves and, before he hops back in the saddle, plants a kiss on his face.

SPORT: GEOCACHER
DOG: SIMON

· · · · ·

Somewhere out there in the woods, schoolyards, parks, and abandoned outlet malls of north Texas,
a black and white Great Dane makes tracks after Tupperware treasures.

He wears red booties, a safety light on his collar, and a backpack stocked with a first-aid kit and doggie knick-knacks (to leave for fellow treasure hunters). At his side is Mandy Hall, who picks her steps carefully, checking her position with a handheld Global Positioning System. They are geocaching—using satellites to pinpoint the location of hidden caches (often a log book and trinkets) hidden just about anywhere you can imagine.

Simon is a bit of a Boy Scout (Dog Scout, actually) and overachiever. It's not enough that he stands 33 inches high at his shoulders and tips the scales at more than 100 pounds. Or that he's candy-cane sweet despite a puppyhood in an abusive home. Or that he bounced back from two painful shoulder surgeries to become the sort of dog that gives more horizontally-

inclined pooches a bad name.

There's more. Simon is a certified AKC Canine Good Citizen and has earned his Companion Dog and Rally Novice Obedience titles. He's been a Delta Society Pet Partner for three years and he's earned badges from the Dog Scouts of America in first aid, dog care and maintenance, rally obedience, backpacking therapy dog, travel safety, and, of course, geocaching.

All of which makes him the ideal friend in need. During a geocaching outing in Beaver's Bend, Oklahoma, Mandy's GPS temporarily stopped working in the middle of nowhere. She says she didn't panic because of big, warm Simon at her side. "There's no other way I would have gone to some of the places I've gone by myself," she says. "No way."

SPORT: WATER AEROBICIZER
DOG: NIKO

• • • • •

As a rule, dogs love naps. They take gold in the sleep Olympics and have advanced degrees in couchology. But not Niko. The carefree, Brittany-born Bouvier des Flandres turned five before he'd steal even a wink during the day. And who can blame him? Life with the Hollingers and Bouvier pals Sherman, Piper, Shadowfax, and Kona was one big derby.

In addition to regular walks, ball, and Frisbee, the pack of downsized Chewbaccas played Chase the Primate. In the woods behind their Virginia home, Bill and Vonie Hollinger and son Billy would tear off in opposite directions and hide, inciting the Bouviers into marathons of tracking and herding until everyone was accounted for. (Primate escapes were encouraged.) Bill, the favorite "prey," bought the house next door so they'd have more land for the game and two-way radios to give the primates a strategic edge.

From May through November, though, athletics shifted to the pool—essentially the dogs' domain. Niko devoured the water with a full-throttle dive followed by hours of random splashing. Like a child, he stayed in the water well after he was cold. By the end of a season of chlorine and sun, his charcoal gray fur faded to silver. Along with his buddies, Niko also played a sort of canine Marco Polo. "It clearly had rules," Bill says, speaking in the past tense, since Niko, the last of his Bouvier clan, died in January, "But I never figured out just what they were."

If Bill went in the house during pool time, Niko and company would stare in the windows—begging him to return, which he invariably did. "They are full of what the French call *joie de vivre*," Bill says. "Being with them infused that joy of life into me."

SPORT: **SANDBAR DASHER**
DOG: **GOOGLY**

· · · · ·

On warm, sunny days
when the tide goes out on the Samish River,
Lea and Jim Lucky clap their hands loudly and shout
at their pit bull, "LET'S GO SWIMMING!"

It's startling the first time you hear it. But the thirteen-year-old Googly, who is almost completely deaf as well as blind, takes the cue as if it was whispered. Then she pads her way down a narrow ramp to the dock. "She has to be the first one there," Lea says.

Once her faded yellow floatation vest is secure, she steps daintily onto an old sailboard, which has no sail. Behind her, Lea straddles the board and rows gently. Googly pitches forward tentatively on the bow as she noses the air—smelling oyster beds, migrating salmon, the breeze off Puget Sound. Her legs are bowed. She suffers arthritis in her joints.

Truth is, Googly is no big fan of swimming. She even seems annoyed when water off Lea's paddle drips on her head. But about twenty minutes downstream, the sailboard fin catches in mud with a shudder. In an instant, Googly transforms. She launches herself onto the ground with abandon. This temporary island is her one safe haven—a soft, smelly sandbar bounded by briny water and free of dangerous obstacles. For a brief spell, she can explore the world at full tilt.

SPORT: ROCK CLIMBERS
DOGS: BISKIT & FELIX

• • • • •

A little mountain goat without the horns,
Biskit didn't so much climb as power her way up serious vertical, finding
paw-holds and muscling skyward as her nails scratched on rock.

She chimneyed up cracks working her back as well as her legs, and when things got sketchy, she summoned her Jack Russell tenacity and grinded to the summit.

But sometimes the tough-minded, free-hand Betty with white wiry fur and brown patches on her ears, eyes, and rump, found herself in tough spots, including one climb that required she rappel 150 feet in a makeshift harness. "She was terrorized, but there was no other way to get her down," says Tom Kelly, who introduced his dog to the sport in the canyons around Boulder, Colorado.

One spring a few years ago, Biskit wandered away from her posse and into the path of a mountain lion. That time, there was no one around to help.

Her spirit and sense of adventure, however, live on in her son Felix. Although he learned to climb in his mother's pawprints, he developed his own dashing style. While Biskit usually discovered the easiest route, Felix (with a rakish brown patch over one eye) bolts straight up. He's less a finesse climber and more a leaper—soaring from base to base. He's athletic, sturdy, and, at just shy of twenty pounds, on the big side for his breed. He also runs long distances, swims rough rivers, and loves chasing critters (true to his fox-hunting genetics). The time he went eye-to-knee with an enormous buck, he caught a hoof in the side but walked away unfazed.

SPORT: GRASS ROLLERS
DOGS: AMOS & OLIVER

• • • • •

Famous Amos of Seattle and his brother Oliver
Wendell Bones walk like they have cement in their heads.

They sniff the ground and rely on their large, low-hanging ears to sweep the aromatic universe into the complex olfactory processing plant we call a nose. When the beagles come across something especially delicious, warm, and pungent in the summer sun, they'll rub their heads in it and let their bodies follow. Then they roll and roll.

And roll some more.

Like wolves over the millennia, they let their short tricolor coats pick up the tang of the invader cats, possums, and raccoons that crisscross the yard under the cover of night.

The twelve-year-old littermates have trained their housemates Anne Croghan and Darlene Barr to open the door to this wonderfully odorous backyard with a mere rap on a bell. But the tall grass in a nearby Seattle park is equally sensational. Amos and Oliver bound across uncut meadows, breaching and diving into the scent-covered blades, the white tips of their tails visible in the distance like tracking flags.

SPORT: BACKPACKER
DOG: HANK

• • • • •

When Val Bate met Hank, he was eighty-two pounds
of ill-mannered exuberance. He avoided eye contact, dragged her
across a parking lot, and snapped his choke chain. Still, she was drawn to
the boisterous German shepherd-rottweiler mix.

As one of ten shelter dogs with less than promising adoption outlooks, Hank "volunteered" for a Portland, Oregon, veterinary technology program, where he and his canine cohorts helped aspiring vet techs including Val learn how to examine a dog, draw blood, and assist with spay and neuter surgery. The furry deputies almost always find a permanent home in the process. Taking a page from Pygmalion, Val decided she'd work with Hank—bringing him on walks and, eventually, hikes—with an eye toward making him more presentable to a future family. Out in the woods, Val and her husband Brian fell in love with the happy-go-lucky dog, and ended up adopting him themselves.

For his part, Hank (whose "official" name is now Henry Wilson Bartholomew Bridges Bates, Herder of Goats, Flusher of Grouse, Earl of Long Tongue) has turned into a bit of an Outward Bounder. He carries his own gear in a backpack, picks huckleberries, responds to a variety of whistle calls, and digs his own bed, though he prefers Val's sleeping bag. His style, though, is still full-bore. He yo-yos up and down trails, soars over logs, and crashes through streams—always with an ear-to-ear grin. If there's snow on the ground, fuggedaboutit!

Hank's attitude is pretty much: *Nothing can stop me.*

SPORT: CART CYCLIST
DOG: MANGO

• • • • •

Peek into most bicycle trailers and usually you'll find a bag of groceries or a shiny-faced toddler. Lift the rain flap on Meredith Rose's rig and you'll be greeted by the salmon-colored nose, golden eyes, folded ears, and perennially furrowed brow of Mango.

The stray pit bull puppy landed in Meredith's life and emergency room when she suffered a femoral fracture courtesy of a car bumper. Meredith, a vet tech, helped nurse Mango through a leg amputation and eventually adopted her. Once she got her home, she realized that making life fun for her dog required a little ingenuity. In order to sneak in quality time with Mango (who often just goes by the lovingly bestowed "Pig"), Meredith brings her to work on a bicycle built for two.

She jury-rigged the trailer with an extra-long mount to make it easier for Mango to get into and out of with only three legs. Unfortunately, the extension adds a degree of difficulty to cornering and other maneuvers on city streets.

But it's worth it. While other dogs stay at home, Mango weaves through traffic in a modern-day rickshaw like a dog out of Horatio Alger.

SPORT: SKI PUNCHER
DOG: JOJO

· · · · ·

JoJo can't trot through the White Salmon Day Lodge
without some hubbub. Doors swing open for her and a chorus of JoJo!s
ripples through the dining room, ski shop, and offices.

As constant companion to Mount Baker Ski Area general manager Duncan Howat, JoJo has guarded the lodge and patrolled the runs for most of her fourteen years. A black and white Border collie with a sweet face and "eye" (the direct stare that makes herding dogs so dang effective), she grew up on the hill and treats the ski area as her own. In spryer days, she'd be everywhere on the mountain at once, zipping between day lodges on a lark. She'd ride up chairlifts and leg down slopes full throttle. All day. "When she was first around snowboarders, I had a tough time stopping her from herding them," Duncan says.

JoJo is slowing down. Though she still loves cross-country hikes through frosty woods and to ride in Duncan's lap as he snowmobiles on his appointed rounds, she cherishes her naps and is not above accepting a cheeseburger—pickles included.

But she's no pushover. She's still a tough-as-nails, triple-alpha female. If Duncan is away during one of the frequent storms that dump more than 50 feet of snow on Washington's North Cascades, JoJo hunkers down in front of the lodge waiting for the sound of his snowmobile or truck. Even in a blizzard, buried in snow, she won't be moved until Duncan returns.

SPORT: SKATEJORER
DOG: NISHA

• • • • •

*Nisha was the "runt" of the litter—a tiny white ball of fur,
not much bigger than a bag of cotton balls—that her Michigan
breeders deemed less-than-promising.*

"They thought she was worthless for sled purposes," says Aaron Wiehe, who got her for a song nine years ago while in his final semester at Purdue University. For a time it looked like Nisha would never fulfill her husky destiny. Still, life was good. After Aaron graduated, they packed up his CJ7 bikini-top Jeep for a summer of camping and rock climbing. Once they moved to Seattle, the mountains beckoned for days of hiking and climbing and snowshoeing.

But as Aaron settled into urban life, he realized that a working dog weaned on days in the backcountry needed a more demanding workout. Walking around neighborhoods just didn't cut it. Aaron decided to channel the desire to pull that is in Nisha's DNA. After some trial and error with a bicycle, he configured a streamlined solution: skateboard, leash, and, on rainy days, an umbrella.

Of course, skatejoring is not without risks. Unlike a dogsled, a skateboard has no brakes, which can pose problems when a springy-legged husky full of energy hears the call of wild.

SPORT: FRISBEE PLAYER
DOG: RIPLEY

• • • • •

Some dogs have the looks. Some dogs have the moves.
Some have both. Meet Ripley. She stops traffic (not just an expression)
in her Madison Heights, Michigan, hometown with her lean, sinewy body,
rusty-gold fur, and Cleopatra ears.

But the real show happens at the park when Mary and Jay Foreman launch a powder blue rubber Frisbee. As it sails through the air, Ripley (a.k.a. BooBoo, Poopala, Dr. Wiggles, Nerd, Stompy, CrazyFace, Wags, Slim, Stretch, and Space Cadet) breaks into a run that could make a rocket jealous.

"She loves her Frisbee more than anything," Jay says about the four-year-old Vizsla. "She lights up. She never wants to stop, and she almost never misses it."

The real trick, though, more impressive than her ability to tear like a roadrunner and vault into the air, is the way she stops. At Jay or Mary's command, she reigns in her pursuit. You can almost hear brakes screeching. It's essential for keeping her out of harm's way when she makes an all-out dash. Her blend of *esprit* and obedience seduces the most died-in-the-wool dog-skeptics. Even Mary's mother, who suffered a lifelong fear of dogs, came to trust and love Ripley. That may have been her biggest catch of all.

SPORT: BOULDERER
DOG: VINCENT THOMAS PUG

• • • • •

First Lieutenant Vincent Thomas Pug (known to family and friends as Vinny the Pug)
took his first scrambling steps into the record books in the summer of 2001.

Transfixed by the rocky landscape (and confused by the cacti) around his new Arizona home, the Orlando-born puppy attempted to scale a boulder with his 6-inch legs. Denied the summit, he tried again and, putting the "pug" in pugnacious, he made it. "To us they are rocks, but to him they are mountains," says Allen Kimble, Vinny's trainer, photographer, biographer, and publicist. For about a year, the silver, snubnosed mountaineer returned to his favorite rock working on technique and conditioning. Since then, he's topped hundreds of boulders in the Phoenix and Sedona areas.

He takes it very aggressively. When Allen says "Up!" Vinny lunges. "I have to be careful because he trusts me and he'll climb on anything I tell him," Allen says. It can be sketchy because Vinny prefers boulders that come to a point, as if he knows that perched on a Matterhorn-like peak with his harness, ropes, and carabiners, he looks like a Swiss mountain guide. Conspicuous on his collar are Allen's own dog tags (he's a Vietnam veteran) and other military insignia, in honor of Allen's daughter who served in Afghanistan and his son-in-law who served in Iraq.

Vinny is probably the world's first and only pug rock climber and he's certainly the most photographed—8,000 images and counting. Every time he reaches a summit, Vinny goes all majestic and Allen clicks. Together they are working toward another record (and raising money for pet rescue along the way): the first dog to have his entire life atop boulders captured for posterity.

SPORT: **WINDSURFER**
DOG: **NINA**

· · · · ·

*People often say, "My dog picked me." If that's true, you have to credit Nina
with excellent powers of selection. The fuzzy golden stray was so nervous in a Portland shelter
that she wasn't allowed in the public meet-up room. But when Lynn Lestock visited
her kennel to get acquainted, Nina crawled into her lap.*

Maybe she smelled Columbia River mud in Lynn's sandals or recognized a kindred water girl—whatever the reason, the puppy's anxiety evaporated like rain on a sun-drenched sail. "Nina wanted to go everywhere with me," Lynn says, which inevitably led to the water. A windsurfer for twenty-five years and former member of the U.S. Olympic windsurfing team, Lynn didn't object when Nina hopped on her board one calm afternoon.

"She just loves to be out there. She looks at the water. She looks at the sky. Her little ears fly," says Lynn, who has never crossed tacks with another windsurfing dog.

"If there are pelicans hanging out on a boat, we'll go around and she barks at them. It's so much fun for me, watching her get such a kick out of it."

Nina, who is named after a friend's wooden boat, is a small golden retriever with mixed heritage that shows up in her narrow nose and curly tail. She and Lynn divide the year between the wind-caressed waters of Oregon's Columbia River Gorge and the Sea of Cortez off the Baja Peninsula, where Lynn manages a windsurfing resort. "She's been a very lucky girl," Lynn says. "I'd like to come back in my next life as her."

SPORT: GEAR TESTER
DOG: OTIS

• • • • •

Patrick Kruse named his dog Otis after a respected babysitter from his youth. That Otis was deaf and had lost a leg in World War II, but still managed to challenge the kids to kick fights.

His four-pawed namesake—an Australian cattle dog with a blue merle coat and black bandit mask—is no fighter, but he's smart, strong willed, and has a big appetite for life. All of which makes the 53-pounder an ideal outdoor companion and gear tester for the founder of Ruff Wear, outfitter to dogs on the go.

Otis is merciless with samples in the Bend, Oregon shop: gnawing on nylon throwing disks and rubber toys, teeth worn down from a lifetime of chomping sticks and pinecones. He has put booties through their paces on mountain-bike trails and cross-country ski treks. He's test-proven backpacks and used the K-9 First-Aid Kit after being bitten in the ear by a buddy named Buddy. But his most important contribution may have been in inspiring the Float Coat.

When Otis was younger, he often would climb into a white-water kayak, riding on the spray skirt, while Patrick paddled. He even made several first river descents by a dog. One drop on the upper North Fork of the Kaweah River in California is named Otis's Slide. Although fishermen love to rib Patrick that a dog in a lifejacket must not be able to swim, the seasoned paddler knows that even the strongest swimmer can be pulled under.

At twelve years old, Otis now prefers to visit Patrick in calm pools and run the shore during the rapids (slowed a bit by ACL surgery).

When Patrick paddles into canyons, he'll look up to see his dog, hundreds of feet above. "There's Otis, looking over the rim and keeping an eye on me. I feel like I'm in the movies. It's like cowboys and Indians."

SPORT: SNORKELER
DOG: BULL

· · · · ·

*The hillside behind Gary Michelson's Los Angeles villa is crowded with
rare, tropical fruits and flowers threaded by an enormous man-made waterfall.
Anchoring this exotic and glamorous garden is Bull.*

A ninety-five-pound American pit bull terrier with a square head, green eyes, and a buckskin coat, Bull lounges poolside like a canine Johnny Weissmuller. Always nearby is his best pal, a sleek rescue whippet named Gracie. Bull packs star power. The muscles in his body show breeding that includes a weight-pull champion grandmother named Dragon. But Bull's talents are less traditional. He uses all that strength to power himself underwater.

When Gary throws a faux cinderblock in the pool, Bull is up like a shot. He watches the toy sink, circles around to the stairs, takes a step, and dives under. Eyes open, he plummets to the deeps for his prize. When the water is warm enough, he'll stay below, swimming along the bottom with his forelegs drawn in and paddling with his back feet. It's uncanny how much he looks like a seal.

That dog needs an agent.

SPORT: SOCCER FORWARD
DOG: HOWIE

• • • • •

Behold Howie, the canine Pelé!
Insert disbelieving eye-roll here. After all, Howie has short legs
and an ample, tube-shaped body. He likes to wear his fleece pullover inside.
In his four-dachshund pack, he's the prissy one.

But watch his determination and grace with a soccer ball and suddenly a new kid's movie comes to mind wherein the Brazilian king of football is trapped in the body of a twelve-year-old persnickety pup.

The black and brown, smooth-coated miniature dachshund channels generations of badger hunters into his one-on-one contest with the ball. He nose dribbles across open spaces, stopping only momentarily to tear at the ball's plastic outer layer. (An effort made difficult by the absence of bottom front teeth.) On a smooth beach, he can really cruise and keeps at it for so many hours he's been known to get sick from all the sand he swallows.

Howie's path to soccer greatness, or at least total soccer ball obsession, was as bumpy as the ground at the Redmond, Washington, park where he practices give-and-goes with Mali McGolden. Her partner, Dani Baker, rescued Howie at two from a home where he'd been treated roughly. At five, he ruptured a disc in his spine, leaving his hind legs paralyzed. Only twenty-four hours after he was diagnosed, Dani agreed to pricey surgery followed by six months crate-recovery with no guarantees. "The fact that he is even able to walk is a miracle," Dani says. "Let alone run like a maniac and play soccer."

SPORT: **SKATEBOARDER**
DOG: **SUNNY**

• • • • •

When Tom Huber was about seven years old, he brought home a stray dog and hid it in his backyard. He hoped that a longstanding parental prohibition against Canis familiarus *might magically be lifted.*

He was wrong. It would be thirty years before Tom could bring a dog home for good. The wait was worth it. Enter Sunny, named for that bright star's positive vibrations. The spirited six-year-old Jack Russell terrier is the little Kahuna of Imperial Beach and master of the beachy arts, from skateboarding and cycling to pickup soccer and rodent hunting. Sunny goes anywhere and everywhere with his welder-artist beach-buddy, often perched on his shoulders. Like a fur stole, Sunny balances while Tom strolls, skateboards, or pedals his funky one-speed through sea foam.

Sunny is agile and intelligent and therefore not always content to merely shoulder-float through life. Tom built him a custom skateboard out of a 6-foot oak plank with a no-skid surface on top, which they share. When a dog-friendly surf-a-thon came to his hometown, Sunny gamely launched into the waves without so much as a tryout.

Now he's mastering one more seaside challenge, balancing on Tom's shoulders while he surfs.

SPORT: BALL WRANGLER
DOG: HOLLY

• • • • •

For two people who don't play tennis, Carol and Martin Beebee have an awful lot of tennis balls. "Our house is littered with them. Our backyard has balls. All the cars have balls. Balls are everywhere," Carol Beebee says.

"I will drive miles to a store if we don't have a ball. Must not ever be without a ball."

The only thing nearly as important as balls is the "zinger," the plastic ball-launcher with which they catapult the fuzzy green orbs into the stratosphere to feed Holly's hearty appetite.

The six-year-old golden retriever with feathery blond fur has plucked tattered Penns and Wilsons from sand drifts in the Great Sand Dunes of Colorado, snow mounds in the High Sierra, San Diego surf, leafy groves in the Smokey Mountains, and rivers from Georgia to Oregon. She runs balls down. She buries them. Digs them up. Hoards them. Hides them. Admires them.

For most of Holly's life, Carol was a travel nurse, which meant she did three-month stints at different hospitals around the country. She and her husband, photographer Martin Beebee, chose locations based on Holly's preferences. Recently they settled in Placerville, California, midway between Sacramento and Lake Tahoe, where an abundance of rivers, mountains, and national forests provide acres of nature for Holly's ball-centric frolics.

"It's all about having a happy dog," Carol explains. "Because, as my husband says, if the dog is happy, his wife is happy. And if his wife is happy, then he'll be happy. So if the dog is happy, the whole family is happy."

SPORT: KAYAKER
DOG: GYPSY DUDE

• • • • •

*When Gypsy Dude wants a lift, he taps his forepaw on the river's edge
like it's a drum until Jim Pytel rows his kayak over. Then the seven-year-old
black Lab shimmies his rear and back legs onto the neoprene spray skirt around
Jim's waist and rests his front paws on the hull.*

He maneuvers with *Matrix*-like agility, keeping his head down while Jim power strokes the boat into a trough. Once they are riding the waves, Gypsy can stand up and enjoy the ride.

"He has gotten so exuberant about it, I have to push him off," says Jim, a twelve-year white-water veteran. "There are certain rivers that you don't want to have a dog on because there is a dangerous rapid or it's really cold—but he still wants to get out there."

Jim bought Gypsy from a farmer in Indiana, when he was four months into a yearlong kayak odyssey. Like something out of *Travels with Charlie* meets *Fear Factor*, they traveled the country in a gear-jammed van, hitting juicy rivers from upstate New York to Tennessee to California, all the way up to British Columbia. That's how Gypsy got his name. Since pretty much everybody calls him "The Dude," though it evolved into Gypsy" Dude.

Today, Gypsy is a little more of a homebody in White Salmon, Washington, where he lives near a waterfall and regularly hikes, plays Frisbee, and kayaks. He also spends a fair amount of time as a solar-powered dog rug.

SPORT: TEAM PLAYERS
DOG: CAMP K9 KIN

· · · · ·

Arna Dan Isacsson shares her one-room cabin in Fairbanks with twenty dogs, give or take new arrivals or those who have left for permanent homes. Many of them are husky mixes, who were abandoned as too small, too old, too stubborn, or too weak. Apparently any reason will do.

"Everybody knows, if you have a last-chance dog, send it to Arna's camp because she has that healing of the hounds," Arna says. She strives to support the rehabilitation that she believes happens among the dogs when they're allowed to live as a group. Her co-counselor is a twelve-year-old Siberian husky named Keetna.

Arna's credo is that love isn't a substitute for outdoor exertion. She takes her "flock" (from the Swedish for *pack*) out to hike, run, swim, walk, skijor, bikejor, boatjor, mush, pick berries, and play chase. On hot summer days, the gang plays "bog ball," an Arna invention that involves running, ball tossing, falling, and generally getting soaked in a cool swamp.

The self-taught skijorer from Sweden often takes

off most of March from her job, so she can take the dogs on epic outings across the snow-covered tundra of central Alaska. They travel in a convoy. Ten to twelve huskies pull a sled. A German shepherd hauls a pulk with dog coats or straw. A Border collie scouts the trail. Others, including a pit bull mix and an Australian shepherd, run behind carrying packs with emergency gear, extra hats and gloves, or dog booties. Everyone has a job.

Arna prefers to rest in the sun and travel at twilight, when the cool air kicks the dogs into overdrive. That's when everything falls into place. She says, "Moving through nature together is a great way to get back to the primal relationship between humans and dogs."

SPORT: DOCK DIVER
DOG: COUNTRY

· · · · ·

It's fair to say few, if any, people saw championship stuff in Country. The lanky, tall coffee-milkshake of a dog had four owners before he turned two. Kevin Meese was number five, and he received Country as a "gift" from a friend when the dog came in dead-last at a coondog field trial in Ohio.

Ever optimistic, Kevin took Country to his home in Fredericktown, Pennsylvania, and dedicated himself to the rangy pup. Country continued to perform toward the back of the pack, until one day in a race through water, Kevin spied something special. "Country would jump over all the dogs when they started," he says. "And then they'd all pass him up." He relished the leap and had bounce, but he couldn't swim. As far as Kevin knew, a leaping skill didn't count for much.

Then, the lightbulb. A few years ago, Kevin saw a televised contest featuring dogs sprinting down a 40-foot dock and sailing into the water. "Country can do that," he told his wife. So he took his seventy-five-pound hound—bred to tree raccoons and track scents—into a competition dominated by water dogs. Four months later, Country racked up three dock-diving distance records in a single day. He went on to be the national Dock Dog Big Air Champion two years in a row—with a current record leap of 28 feet, 10 inches. He also snatched an Extreme Vertical National Championship with a 7-foot, 8-inch high jump, which means he would have cleared Shaquille O'Neal's head by 7 inches.

Some folks point to Country's conditioning as the source of his spring. But it's probably Kevin's consistent doting that gives the champ a reason to jump for joy.

SPORT: INNERTUBER
DOG: RIA

• • • • •

Open water constitutes one of the main ingredients in bliss for most
Labrador retrievers. (Naps and treats are a close second.) So when one of their number
joins a family dedicated to water-based pleasures, life's looking pretty good.

It gets even better when that dog—a chocolaty delight named Ria—figures out how to kick back in lagoons and lakes in an innertube. "She does what we do," says Laura LeDesky, who along with husband Terry and daughter Elisa has splashed away the summers with Ria for eight years. "She saw us hanging out in the innertube and thought, 'well, why can't I? I'm going to hang out too.' Pretty soon it was her innertube." (She took that same "me too!" attitude toward kids wooshing down slides at a local playground, but that's another story.)

Ria doesn't lie flat on her back like a kid in a Rockwell painting. Instead, she perches on the inside of the innertube, which sits upright in the water. Her back paws are parked on the tube; her forelegs hang over the front. She looks like a shiny otter trapped inside an enormous donut.

Named after the Spanish word for estuary, Ria is a showstopper wherever she floats—from her hometown pond on Whidbey Island, Washington, to a mountain lake in Bozeman, Montana. She's earned hoots of approval from cliff-jumping teenagers, inquiries from owners who'd like a tubing dog of their own, and cries of "get away!" from strangers in a lake who had no plans to share their air mattress with a dog.

SPORT: FREE-WHEELER
DOG: SKYE

· · · · ·

When Skye cruises the dusty trails outside Boulder, Colorado, she's a sight for sore eyes.
The twelve-year-old Border collie hauls a big stick in her mouth; her backend is suspended
between two fat tires that kick up gravel and glance off rocks like a
souped-up ATV. Don't stop to stare, just get out of the way.

Skye's back legs were paralyzed when she fell out of a willow tree into which she had climbed on a windy, icy December day two years ago. It was a devastating blow for Robert Troup, who wasn't sure the dog he'd followed to the top of 14-foot peaks would romp again.

After unsuccessful outings using a stroller, he bought her a wheelchair. It took Skye about fifteen minutes of bucking and biting before she got it. "I just remember the walk that day: She wagged her tail the entire time," Robert says. Then she set about wrecking the contraption. Out on the range, she rolled it. Banged it into things. Blew out the tires. "I asked them when they made it, 'Is that a heavy-duty chair? Because she's a wild girl,'" Robert says. After six months, he had to get her a new one, which he toughened up with mountain-bike gear for their rugged rambles.

For his part, Robert curbs his bushwhacking tendencies, so the sweet and loyal friend can be included on outings with the pack, which includes her daughter Lucy, a "sister-in-law" Paige, and Paige's daughter Grace. Skye used to be the leader, forging the way ahead. Now the others are up front, but "they still wait for her," Robert says. "And she still administers her justice and will put them in their places."

SPORT: HIKER
DOG: BAILEY

• • • • •

"Whenever I would say, 'Bailey, where are the cows? 'That would set her off,"
says Dave Estep about his creamy white Whippet-mix hiking buddy. It's not that
she loved cows; she loved what cows represented.

When she was a puppy in Raleigh, North Carolina, a small herd grazed at the trailhead of her regular hike, and because she adored nothing more than moving coyote-like up hillsides and over boulders, she yelped excitedly any time she saw cows. She knew the word "cows." She knew how to spell it. Horses, even chubby horses, couldn't trip her up.

On the trail, she was a trustworthy companion. She scouted the route, but always stayed close. She summited peaks in the Cascades and was agile on rocks. She loved camping out—and witnessed at least one serious meteor shower—but after a strenuous day, she wasn't shy about urging Dave to the tent, where she curled up at the foot of his sleeping bag.

The only other thing Bailey liked almost as much as a hike was a cold beer, which she tackled with the same sporting gusto. When someone set down an empty bottle, she would lick the rim and knock it over with her snout. Then she'd take her paw and hold it down. "Her tongue would go in the neck, no kidding, probably like five inches, and she'd be lapping the inside of the bottle," Dave says. She'd scoot the bottle across the room. Then carry it back and start all over. "She was pretty famous for that."

SPORT: SNOW PUNCHER
DOG: LILY

• • • • •

*When a glove disappears from an open garage in a certain Truckee,
California, neighborhood, everyone knows the culprit. A masked bandit
named Lily. But there's no penalty for the robbery.*

Finding and retrieving gloves, hats, and sweaters has been this blue heeler's *raison d'être* for eleven years.

She's the nose and paws of a Squaw Valley avalanche rescue duo that includes ski patroller Matt Calcutt. "For Lily, work is play and play is work," Matt says. Together, they have filled thousands of happy hours searching for articles of clothing and people hidden behind trees in the summer and under snow in the winter—all with the serious aim of quickly locating an avalanche victim. Though she's never found a body, she has discovered signs of humans in avalanche zones.

"She'll do anything I ask her to do," Matt says, including hopping onto a chairlift like a pro and riding with her paws in his lap. Some days for exercise, she runs uphill under the chairlift instead. As one of only two herders among the nine Squaw Valley avalanche dogs, Lily has to work extra hard to curb her desire to round up snowboarders whizzing past. When it's time to ski, she trots between Matt's snowplowing legs. If curious folks try to reach out to Lily, their ski edges could cut her legs. In this position, Matt protects her. A fixture at the resort since she was four months old, Lily is in semi-retirement now. She doesn't tackle backcountry avalanches anymore. But she does still report to work every day of the season, "trains" (or rather, plays) constantly, helps with nearby rescues, and demonstrates to the next generation of avalanche pups the pure joy of finding a glove.

For Denali

Published by Skipstone, an imprint of The Mountaineers Books
Printed in China

First printing 2007
10 09 08 07   5 4 3 2 1

The publisher and author gratefully acknowledge the following photographers (listed in order of first appearance), without whom this book could not have been unleashed:

Pages 2–3, 62–63, Martin Beebee Photography; pages 4, 8–9, 14–15, 18–21, 22–23, 30–31, 34–35, 36–39, 40–41, 42–43, 44–45, 54–57, 58–59, 60–61, 72–73, Bev Sparks; pages 6–7, Thad Allendar; pages 10–11, Chris Noble, www.noblefoto.com; pages 12–13, Adam Stein Photography; pages 16–17, Dick Ross, www.SeeKCRun.com; pages 24–25, Mandy Hall; pages 26–29, Bill Hollinger; page 32, Jonathan Copp; page 33, James C. Ruch; pages 46–47, Ken Steil; pages 48–49, Allen Y. Kimble, Jr. of "Vinny the Pug Enterprises" and "Vinny the Pug Foundation"; pages 50–51, DavidLokey@mac.com; pages 52, 53 (top left), Patrick Kruse/Ruff Wear; page 53 (top right), Mike Houska, Dogleg Studios/Ruff Wear; page 53 (bottom), Kevin Jurgens/Ruff Wear; pages 64–65, Brian Fields; pages 66–69, Charles Mason; pages 70–71, Steven Lankford Photography; pages 74–75, RobertTroupPhotography.com; pages 76–77, Dennis Wise/www.studio3.com; pages 78–79, Keoki Flagg.

Copy Editor: Susan Hodges
Design: Karen Schober
Layout: Jane Jeszeck/www.jigsawseattle.com
Cover photograph: Bev Sparks

ISBN 978-159485-036-3

Library of Congress Cataloging-in-Publication Data

Skipstone books may be purchased for corporate, educational, or other promotional sales. For special discounts and information, contact our Sales Department at 1-800-553-4453 or mbooks@mountaineersbooks.org.

Skipstone
1001 SW Klickitat Way
Suite 201
Seattle, Washington 98134
206.223.6303
www.skipstonepress.org
www.mountaineersbooks.org

SKIPSTONE
LIVE LIFE
MAKE RIPPLES

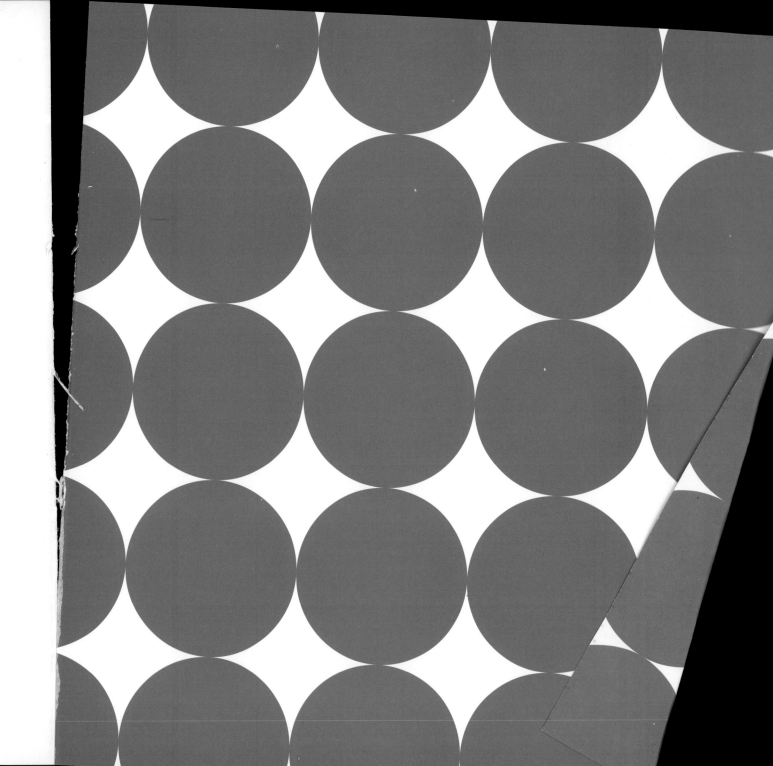